Inventory of Breeding Birds of the Alagnak Wild River

Natural Resource Technical Report NPS/SWAN/NRTR—2012/623

Kelly Walton and Tracey Gotthardt

Alaska Natural Heritage Program
University of Alaska Anchorage
707 A Street
Anchorage, AK 99501

Fieldwork and technical assistance by Tracey Gotthardt, Kelly Walton, Jennifer McGrath and Tamara Fields, Alaska Natural Heritage Program, UAA; Troy Hamon, Katmai National Park and Preserve; and David Tessler, Alaska Department of Fish and Game.

September 2012

U.S. Department of the Interior
National Park Service
Natural Resource Stewardship and Science
Fort Collins, Colorado

The National Park Service, Natural Resource Stewardship and Science office in Fort Collins, Colorado publishes a range of reports that address natural resource topics of interest and applicability to a broad audience in the National Park Service and others in natural resource management, including scientists, conservation and environmental constituencies, and the public.

The Natural Resource Technical Report Series is used to disseminate results of scientific studies in the physical, biological, and social sciences for both the advancement of science and the achievement of the National Park Service mission. The series provides contributors with a forum for displaying comprehensive data that are often deleted from journals because of page limitations.

All manuscripts in the series receive the appropriate level of peer review to ensure that the information is scientifically credible, technically accurate, appropriately written for the intended audience, and designed and published in a professional manner.

This report received informal peer review by subject-matter experts who were not directly involved in the collection, analysis, or reporting of the data.

Views, statements, findings, conclusions, recommendations, and data in this report do not necessarily reflect views and policies of the National Park Service, U.S. Department of the Interior. Mention of trade names or commercial products does not constitute endorsement or recommendation for use by the U.S. Government.

This report is available from the Southwest Alaska I&M Network website (http://science.nature.nps.gov/im/units/SWAN) and the Natural Resource Publications Management website (http://www.nature.nps.gov/publications/nrpm/).

Please cite this publication as:

NPS 193/116866, September 2012

Contents

Contents (continued)

Figures

Tables

Appendices

Abstract

Biologists from the Alaska Natural Heritage Program and the National Park Service conducted an inventory of breeding birds along the Alagnak Wild River (ALAG) during June 2011. We used a stratified random sampling design based on land cover type to insure adequate distribution of sample points throughout all representative landcover classes. To survey for birds, two, two-person crews conducted 71 point count surveys across 9 sampling grids along the Alagnak River corridor. We detected 76 species, including 13 species of conservation concern. Three species detected during this inventory were new to the ALAG bird checklist and included the American Kestrel, Bar-tailed Godwit, and Arctic Warbler. Of the other 73 other species detected, 84% were considered present on the park species list. The most commonly detected species were the Wilson's Warbler, American Tree Sparrow, Savannah Sparrow, and White-crowned Sparrow. These species were also the most widely distributed species at locations where we conducted point counts and were often associated with shrub communities. ALAG is the last southwest Alaska network park to be inventoried for avian fauna. This inventory contributes to the knowledge of the breeding bird community in this region and establishes baseline information on species status for any future monitoring efforts.

Acknowledgments

The following individuals provided invaluable support during completion of this project: We would like to thank Bill Thompson and Michael Shepard, National Park Service, Southwest Area Network, for allocating funding for this project, as well as for providing administrative support and oversight. Troy Hamon and Claudette Moore, Katmai National Park and Preserve, provided valuable information and assistance prior to and during the planning phases of the project. Tamara Fields, Alaska Natural Heritage Program, and Bill Thompson assisted with study design. We are especially grateful to Troy Hamon and David Tessler, Alaska Department of Fish and Game, for their hard work and guidance in the field, and for getting us down the river safely. Jennifer McGrath, Alaska Natural Heritage Program, assisted with data entry and analysis. Tammy Wilson, Southwest Alaska Network, provided valuable comments to prior versions of this report.

Introduction

The National Park Service (NPS) oversees more than 200,000 km^2 of protected lands in Alaska. To provide effective, long-term protection and management within these holdings, NPS established four inventory and monitoring networks: Arctic, Central, Southeast, and Southwest networks. The Southwest Alaska Network (SWAN) consists of the Alagnak Wild River (ALAG), Aniakchak National Monument and Preserve (ANIA), Katmai National Park and Preserve (KATM), Kenai Fjords National Park (KEFJ), and Lake Clark National Park and Preserve (LACL) (Figure 1). In response to the formation of the inventory and monitoring networks and the need for more sound biological information, avian studies have recently been conducted in the majority of the SWAN parks (KEFJ- Van Hemert 2006, KATM and LACL- Ruthrauff et al. 2007, ANIA- Ruthrauff and Tibbitts 2009). ALAG is the only park unit within SWAN that has not been inventoried for avian fauna. An inventory of ALAG will lay the groundwork for park managers to develop effective monitoring programs, make informed management decisions concerning species or their habitats, and to educate the public.

The need for scientific inventory of avian species was outlined by the 2001 NPS Management Policies Act, which tasks the Southwest Alaska Network with acquiring information on the status and trends of selected ecological indicators, within its five NPS units, including ALAG. The only currently available avian list for ALAG (NPSpecies 2008) was compiled based on observations from field notes, park reports (e.g., Savage 1997, McCullogh et al. 1997), and educated guesses. While ALAG is the smallest of the SWAN park units, it preserves the upper 90 km of riverine habitat in a pristine, free-flowing condition as well as the surrounding riparian and upland environment, which are extremely valuable habitats for avian species. The headwaters of the Alagnak River lie within the rugged Aleutian Range in neighboring KATM. The Alagnak River meanders west from KATM traversing the Alaska Peninsula towards Bristol Bay and the Bering Sea on the western coast of Alaska (NPS 2011).

Despite NPS protection, the Alagnak River is not immune to natural or human induced disturbance. Prehistoric people have lived along the Alagnak River as early as 8,000 years ago, leaving behind evidence of their rich subsistence lifestyle. In recent years, the Alagnak River has become the most popular fly-in fishing destination in southwest Alaska. As a result of increased visitation, sport fishing pressure, and resultant wave action from motorboats, riverbank erosion has become a concern along the Alagnak River (NPS 2011). Although unstudied within this river system, undercut banks resulting from motorboat induced erosion can have a direct impact on riparian vegetation and thus, the quality of avian habitats. Additionally, potential development outside the park (i.e. gas and oil development, mineral extraction) could impact the area. Baseline inventories will provide an invaluable tool for assessing anthropogenic impacts, evaluating changes in avian communities to climate change, and assisting with future management decisions.

Objectives

The NPS Alaska Region Science Strategy states that scientific data should guide management decisions for preserving NPS core values within each park (NPS 2006). In response to the NPS need for more information on their avian resources, biologists from the Alaska Natural Heritage Program (AKNHP) and NPS conducted an inventory of breeding birds within ALAG with two principal goals:

1

1. Use targeted river and land surveys during the breeding season to document as many bird species as possible within the Alagnak River corridor.
2. Quantify the distribution, relative abundance, and habitat associations of bird species occurring within ALAG during the breeding season.

To accomplish these objectives, we:

1. Implemented a repeatable, scientifically valid sampling design suited to survey birds in riparian areas with limited access.
2. Collected data on vegetation cover type and physical attributes at each sample point in order to describe avian habitat associations.

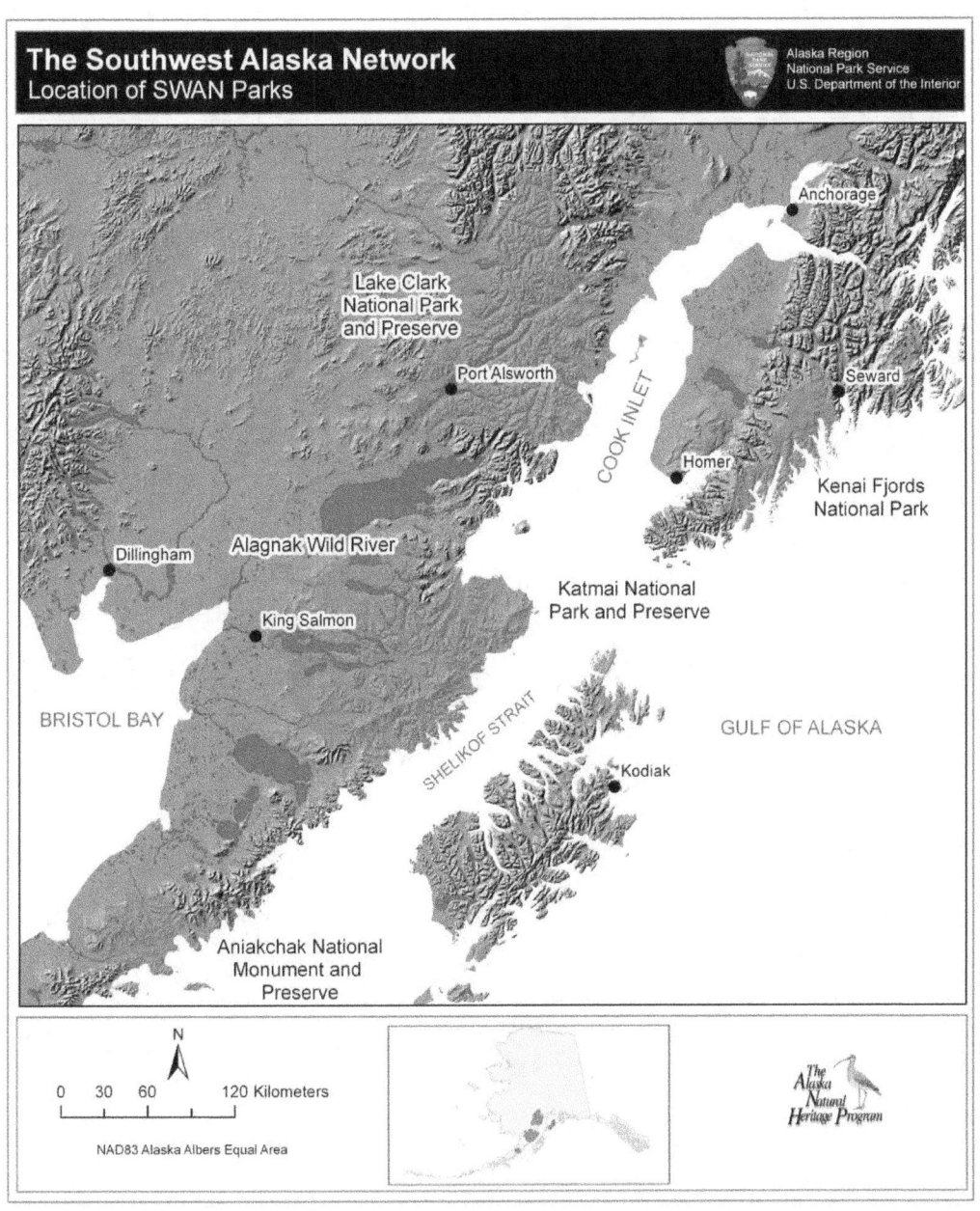

Figure 1. Location of National Parks within the Southwest Alaska Network.

Methods

Spatial Sampling Design Overview

The sampling frame for the ALAG avian inventory included riparian and upland areas that were accessible by raft or on foot and were within federal jurisdiction. To determine the location of sampling sites, we used a stratified random sampling design with strata based on land cover type to insure adequate distribution of sample points throughout all representative land cover classes. The KATM land cover map (NPS 2003) was used to delineate land cover type, except for the lower river which was not covered by the KATM map, where we used the LANDFIRE map (LANDFIRE 1.0.0) instead. To accommodate sampling in a riverine system with a narrow upland boundary, random placement of points was constrained to fit within park boundaries. As a result, sampling grids consisted of eight to eleven points with 250 to 500 m in between, depending on the width of the park boundary and whether or not terrain was open (500 m) or closed (250 m). Following this protocol, 30 sample grids were selected and prioritized for sampling based on their proximity to rare land cover types (Figure 2). Rare land cover types were those that made up a small percentage of the total survey area and therefore were allocated fewer points during stratification. Grids containing points that occurred in rare land cover types were classified as high priority, grids adjacent to high priority sites were considered moderate priority, and the remaining grids were assigned low priority. The resulting sampling frame encompassed approximately 110 km^2 across 17 land cover types in the upper section of the Alagnak River (using the KATM land cover map) and 14 land cover types along the lower section of the river (based on the LANDFIRE map). See Appendix 1 for associated land cover types and the distribution of sampling points.

Field Methods

Surveys were conducted in early June and designed to target birds present during the breeding season. Field personnel consisted of two teams of two people. Field crews were dropped off by floatplane at Kukaklek Lake in KATM and floated approximately 100 kilometers down river to a pick up location just outside of the ALAG boundary. Sample locations were accessed by rafting the Alagnak River corridor and stopping at access points where teams could walk to sampling points. Bird detections were based on ten minute point count surveys, conducted at each point by one observer using distance sampling methodology (Buckland et al. 2001) and the Alaska Landbird Monitoring System (ALMS) protocols (Handel and Cady 2004). These sampling methodologies were selected to be consistent with those used by the KATM, LACL, ANIA, and KEFJ bird inventories in other SWAN parks. The time interval of first detection (0-3 min, 3-5 min, 5-8 min, 8-10 min), species, number of individuals, radial distance from survey point, and behavior, including breeding status indicators, were recorded for each bird detection. Laser rangefinders were used to measure distances to individual birds. If the individual was heard but not seen, we estimated the possible range of its distance. In addition to birds recorded at sampling points, the approximate location and identity of any previously undetected or rare birds encountered during travel between points was also recorded.

Standard site data were recorded at each point, including observer, date, time of day, weather, wind speed and direction, slope, aspect, elevation, latitude and longitude. Vegetation within 50 m of the sampling point was classified to Viereck (et al. 1992) level III. When a mosaic of habitat types existed within the circle, the percent of the circle occupied by each habitat type was recorded. Digital photographs were taken in each cardinal direction at sample points to supplement the habitat data.

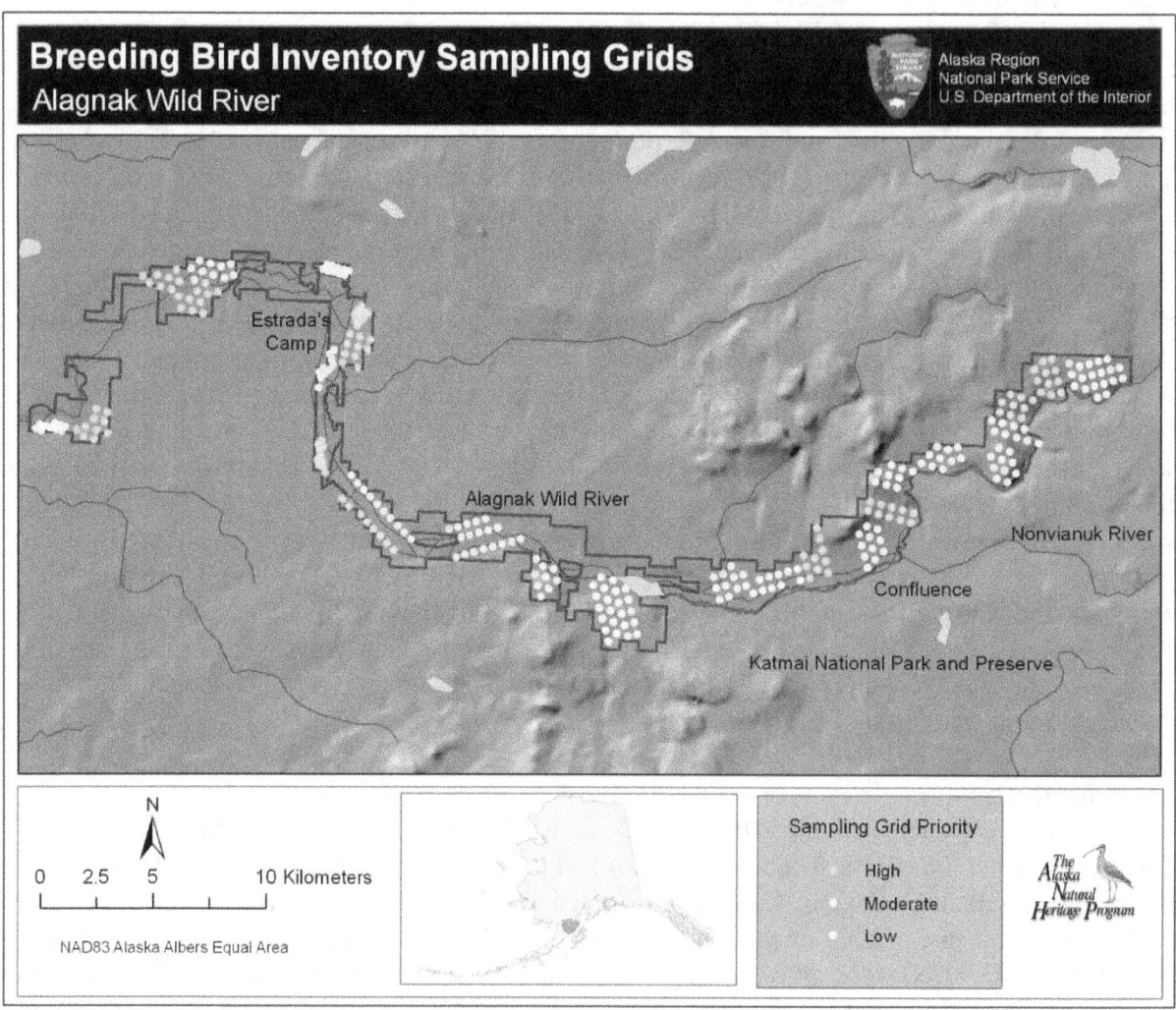

Figure 2. Alagnak Wild River 2011 breeding bird inventory proposed sampling grids colored by priority. The Alagnak Wild River boundary is outlined in red and Katmai National Park and Preserve is shaded in green.

Species List and Species of Conservation Concern

The ALAG NPSpecies bird checklist was compiled by AKNHP (Lenz et al. 2002) and certified in 2007 (NPSpecies 2008). This list details the occurrence of 123 species, of which 74 are listed as present in the ALAG and 49 are listed as probably present in the park. Considering that our work is the first systematic avian survey within the Alagnak Wild River boundary, we used this opportunity to validate the checklist by providing further justification for the occurrence, residency, and abundance of birds.

Within the NPSpecies ALAG bird checklist, we identified species of conservation concern as defined by one of six conservation agencies: Audubon Alaska (Kirchoff and Padula 2010), Partners in Flight (Rich et al. 2004), U S. Fish and Wildlife Service (U.S. Fish and Wildlife

Service 2008), Alaska Shorebird Group (Alaska Shorebird Group 2008), Boreal Partners in Flight (Boreal Partners in Flight Working Group 1999), and AKNHP's conservation status ranks (S1 to S3 and G1 to G3). The criteria for inclusion on each organization's list varied, but in general, species of conservation concern are those with threatened, declining, or small populations.

Species Abundance and Distribution

To obtain a coarse measure of mean bird abundance, we standardized bird counts for survey effort by dividing the number of individuals detected at each point count by the total number of points surveyed for all species detected during the ALAG survey. This calculation yielded mean bird abundance per-point, which we refer to as "average occurrence" to remain consistent with the other SWAN avian inventory reports (Van Hemert 2006, Ruthrauff et al. 2007, Ruthrauff and Tibbitts 2009). As a coarse measure of species distribution, we calculated the percentage of points at which a species was detected. This percent detection calculation, which describes the frequency of occurrence at sample points, was made by dividing the number of points at which a species was detected by the total number of points surveyed.

Given the difficulty in distinguishing between Common and Hoary Redpoll, and in the absence of confirming evidence, we combined observations for all summaries as 'redpoll species'. Based on the known distribution of both species, most were likely Common Redpolls (Knox and Lowther 2000a, 2000b).

Associations Between Birds and Habitats

We used vegetation cover type data collected at each sample point to assess species-habitat associations. We grouped similar vegetation cover types into five broad categories based on the Viereck system (Viereck et al 1992, Appendix 2). The Viereck system identifies vegetation communities in Alaska from the general (level I- gross structural components) to the more specific (species compositions). At level I, primary vegetation types are divided into major classes: forest (> 10% trees), shrub (> 10% dwarf trees or > 25% erect or decumbent shrubs), and herbaceous. At level II, vegetation is further divided based on the types of trees, height of shrubs, and type of herbaceous plants. Level III then divides vegetation based on canopy cover. We lacked sufficient data to conduct our analyses at Viereck level III. Instead, our five cover types were groupings at Viereck level I and II and included needleleaf forest, broadleaf and mixed forest, tall shrub (≥ 1.5 m tall), low and dwarf shrub (1.5 m tall), and herbaceous (graminoids, herbs, mosses, lichens). To assess bird-habitat relationships, we compared the percent cover of habitat types at point count locations to species occurrence data (for species with greater than 10 detections within a 50 meter radius of the point center).

Methodological Limitations

Our primary objective with this study was to conduct an inventory of avian species that use the ALAG during the breeding season, and secondarily, to provide cursory information regarding abundance, distribution and habitat associations which future studies can build upon. Thus, our focus was on providing justification for the existing ALAG bird checklist. We also provided generalized summaries of bird counts, but we did not explicitly account for detection probability, which was beyond the scope of this study.

We recognize that the rough estimates of species abundance and distribution (relying on presence/absence data) presented here are likely biased (Tyre et al. 2003). With a single, brief visit to each point during a rapid inventory, failure to detect a species at a given point does not mean that the species did not occur there or use the associated habitat type during the breeding season. A species may have been present during the time of the survey, but not detected by the observer, or the species could have been absent during the brief count period but used the area at other times as part of its breeding territory (MacKenzie 2005). Accordingly, we likely underestimated the number of sites at which any given species occurred.

Caution should also be used when comparing across species because of differing detectabilities and when comparing within a species across habitats because different habitats also have different detectabilities (Buckland 2006). In most cases, analysis without correcting for detectability will underestimate the effects of habitat on occurrence (Tyre et al. 2003). Any species specific habitat associations that we noted are likely valid, but a detailed understanding of actual species abundance, distribution, and habitat associations is impossible without formally accounting for availability bias and detection bias using advanced analytical procedures (e.g. Tyre et al. 2003, or Royle et al. 2004).

Lastly, we recognize that different species exhibit different behaviors and a single survey method is unlikely to work well across multiple species (Buckland 2006). Our survey was specifically designed to detect landbirds using a point count methodology in terrestrial habitats. While this survey technique is widely used for monitoring trends in abundance of passerines, it has a much lower likelihood of detecting other groups of species (i.e., raptors, grouse, waterfowl, shorebirds, etc…) that are more cryptic in their behaviors or are primarily outside of the targeted habitats, or simply breed outside the survey window (i.e. grouse). We acknowledge that our inventory was biased towards landbird species and that constraints in timing or methodology may have limited the probability of detection of other groups of species.

Results

Survey Effort and Conditions

Avian surveys were conducted along the Alagnak River corridor during June 2-13, 2011. In total, we conducted surveys at 71 points, within 9 different sampling grids across forest, shrub, and herbaceous habitat types. Sampling effort took place over 7 days (not including river travel days) and entailed over 87 hours of survey time.

We surveyed fewer grids (9 vs. 16) than originally planned. The original survey was designed by Tamara Fields (formerly of AKNHP) and Bill Thompson (formerly of NPS), who were not involved on the actual fieldwork. Once field crews were on the ground, we realized the sampling plan was overly ambitious, largely due to the amount of time it took to travel between survey grids via raft along the river. In order to maximize our two week survey window, we selected base camps that were in close proximity to high priority sites, where two high priority grids were adjacent to each other, and where camping was feasible.

Although survey conditions were generally good, we did have one day of inclement weather (high winds) when we were unable to survey. Temperatures during surveys ranged from 7 to 16°C, and approximately 15% of counts were conducted during periods of active precipitation.

Species List

We detected a total of 76 individual species, including 12 species of waterfowl, 1 loon, 7 raptors, 1 crane, 8 shorebirds, 4 gulls and terns, 2 grouse and ptarmigan, 3 owls, 3 woodpeckers, 1 kingfisher, and 34 passerines (Table 1). Forty-nine of the 76 species were detected during point counts and the remaining 29 were detected walking between points, at camp, or on travel days. We detected three species (American Kestrel, Bar-tailed Godwit, and Arctic Warbler) not previously recorded in ALAG. Fourteen species detected during surveys were previously listed as "probably present" on the NPSpecies Alagnak Wild River park checklist. Additionally, we detected evidence of 1 species of amphibian and 11 species of mammals (see Appendix 3 for annotated list).

We detected 13 bird species of conservation concern, including 1 species of grouse, 1 raptor, 4 shorebirds, 1 seabird, 1 owl and 5 passerines (Table 2). An additional 13 species of conservation concern are shown on the NPSpecies list as present or probably present in ALAG. Two of the species we detected have a State Heritage Ranks of one to three (S1-S3), indicating higher conservation concern, including the Bar-tailed Godwit (S3B) and Hudsonian Godwit (S2S3B).

Table 1. Birds of Alagnak Wild River, Alaska (NPSpecies 2008). 'P' indicates a species recorded by a previous observer, 'PP' indicates species is considered probably present, but unconfirmed, and species denoted by an 'X' were detected during the 2011 inventory.

Common Name	Scientific Name	Global Rank[1]	State Rank[1]	Previously Recorded	Recorded in 2011
Waterfowl					
Greater White-fronted Goose	*Anser albifrons*	G5	S5B	P	
Brant	*Branta bernicla*	G5	S4B	P	
Cackling Goose	*Branta hutchinsii*	G5	S5B	PP	
Canada Goose	*Branta canadensis*	G5	S5B	P	
Tundra Swan	*Cygnus columbianus*	G5	S4B	P	X
Gadwall	*Anas strepera*	G5	S4B	PP	
Eurasian Wigeon	*Anas penelope*	G5	S3N	PP	
American Wigeon	*Anas americana*	G5	S4N,S5B	P	X
Mallard	*Anas platyrhynchos*	G5	S5	P	X
Northern Shoveler	*Anas clypeata*	G5	S5B	P	X
Northern Pintail	*Anas acuta*	G5	S5B, S5N	P	
Green-winged Teal	*Anas crecca*	G5	S4N,S5B	P	X
Canvasback	*Aythya valisineria*	G5	S4B	PP	
Redhead	*Aythya americana*	G5	S3S4B	PP	
Greater Scaup	*Aythya marila*	G5	S5B,S5N	P	X
Harlequin Duck	*Histrionicus histrionicus*	G4	S4B, S4N	P	X
Surf Scoter	*Melanitta perspicillata*	G5	S4B,S4N	P	
Black Scoter	*Melanitta americana*	G5	S3S4B, S3N	PP	
Long-tailed Duck	*Clangula hyemalis*	G5	S5B, S4N	P	X
Bufflehead	*Bucephala albeola*	G5	S5B, S5N	PP	
Common Goldeneye	*Bucephala clangula*	G5	S4N, S5B	P	X
Barrow's Goldeneye	*Bucephala islandica*	G5	S5B, S5N	P	X
Hooded Merganser	*Lophodytes cucullatus*	G5	S3B	PP	
Common Merganser	*Mergus merganser*	G5	S5B	P	X
Red-breasted Merganser	*Mergus serrator*	G5	S5B, S5N	P	X
Grouse and Ptarmigan					
Spruce Grouse	*Falcipennis canadensis*	G5	S5	P	X
Willow Ptarmigan	*Lagopus lagopus*	G5	S5	P	X
Rock Ptarmigan	*Lagopus muta*	G5	S5	PP	
Loons and Grebes					
Red-throated Loon	*Gavia stellata*	G5	S4B, S4N	PP	
Pacific Loon	*Gavia pacifica*	G5	S5B, S4N	PP	
Common Loon	*Gavia immer*	G5	S5B, S4N	P	X
Horned Grebe	*Podiceps auritus*	G5	S4S5B, S4N	P	
Red-necked Grebe	*Podiceps grisegena*	G5	S4S5B,S4N	PP	
Seabirds					

Common Name	Scientific Name	Global Rank[1]	State Rank[1]	Previously Recorded	Recorded in 2011
Fork-tailed Storm Petrel	Oceanodroma furcata	G5	S5B, S4N	P	
Raptors					
Osprey	Pandion haliaetus	G5	S3S4B	P	X
Bald Eagle	Haliaeetus leucocephalus	G5	S5	P	X
Northern Harrier	Circus cyaneus	G5	S4B	P	X
Sharp-shinned Hawk	Accipiter striatus	G5	S4B,S3N	PP	
Northern Goshawk	Accipiter gentilis	G5	S4	PP	X
Rough-legged Hawk	Buteo lagopus	G5	S4B	P	
Merlin	Falco columbarius	G5	S5B, S4N	P	X
American Kestrel	Falco sparverius	G5	S4B		NEW
Gyrfalcon	Falco rusticolus	G5	S4	PP	
Peregrine Falcon	Falco peregrinus	G4	S3B, S3N	PP	X
Cranes					
Sandhill Crane	Grus canadensis	G5	S5B	P	X
Shorebirds					
Black-bellied Plover	Pluvialis squatarola	G5	S4B	P	
American Golden-plover	Pluvialis dominica	G5	S5B	PP	
Pacific Golden-plover	Pluvialis fulva	G5	S4B	PP	
Semipalmated Plover	Charadrius semipalmatus	G5	S5B	PP	X
Spotted Sandpiper	Actitis macularius	G5	S5B	P	X
Greater Yellowlegs	Tringa melanoleuca	G5	S5B	P	X
Lesser Yellowlegs	Tringa flavipes	G5	S5B	P	X
Whimbrel	Numenius phaeopus	G5	S3S4B	P	X
Hudsonian Godwit	Limosa haemastica	G4	S2S3B	PP	X
Bar-tailed Godwit	Limosa lapponica	G5	S3B		NEW
Ruddy Turnstone	Arenaria interpres	G5	S4B	P	
Least Sandpiper	Calidris minutilla	G5	S5B	P	
Short-billed Dowitcher	Limnodromus griseus	G5	S4S5B	P	
Wilson's Snipe	Gallinago delicata	G5	S5B	P	X
Red-necked Phalarope	Phalaropus lobatus	G4G55	S4S5B	PP	
Red Phalarope	Phalaropus fulicarius	G5	S4S5B	PP	
Gulls, Terns, Jaegers					
Bonaparte's Gull	Chroicocephalus philadelphia	G5	S5B	P	X
Mew Gull	Larus canus	G5	S5B	P	X
Glaucous-winged Gull	Larus glaucescens	G5	S5	P	X
Glaucous Gull	Larus hyperboreus	G5	S5B,S4N	PP	
Black-legged Kittiwake	Rissa tridactyla	G5	S5B, S5N	PP	
Arctic Tern	Sterna paradisaea	G5	S4S5B	P	X
Parasitic Jaeger	Stercorarius parasiticus	G5	S5B	PP	
Long-tailed Jaeger	Stercorarius longicaudus	G5	S5B	PP	

Common Name	Scientific Name	Global Rank[1]	State Rank[1]	Previously Recorded	Recorded in 2011
Owls					
Great Horned Owl	*Bubo virginianus*	G5	S5	P	
Snowy Owl	*Bubo scandiacus*	G5	S3S4	PP	
Northern Hawk Owl	*Surnia ulula*	G5	S5	PP	X
Short-eared Owl	*Asio flammeus*	G5	S4B	P	X
Boreal Owl	*Aegolius funereus*	G5	S4	PP	X
Northern Saw-whet Owl	*Aegolius acadicus*	G5	S3	PP	
Hummingbirds, Kingfishers					
Rufous Hummingbird	*Selasphorus rufus*	G5	S4B	PP	
Belted Kingfisher	*Megaceryle alcyon*	G5	S5	P	X
Woodpeckers					
Downy Woodpecker	*Picoides pubescens*	G5	S5	P	X
Hairy Woodpecker	*Picoides villosus*	G5	S5	PP	X
American Three-toed Woodpecker	*Picoides dorsalis*	G5	S5	P	X
Passerines					
Olive-sided Flycatcher	*Contopus cooperi*	G4	S4S5B	P	
Alder Flycatcher	*Empidonax alnorum*	G5	S5B	P	X
Northern Shrike	*Lanius excubitor*	G5	S4B,S4N	PP	
Gray Jay	*Perisoreus canadensis*	G5	S5	P	X
Black-billed Magpie	*Pica hudsonia*	G5	S5	P	X
Common Raven	*Corvus corax*	G5	S5	P	X
Tree Swallow	*Tachycineta bicolor*	G5	S5B	P	X
Violet-green Swallow	*Tachycineta thalassina*	G5	S5B	PP	
Bank Swallow	*Riparia riparia*	G5	S5B	P	X
Black-capped Chickadee	*Poecile atricapillus*	G5	S5	P	X
Boreal Chickadee	*Poecile hudsonica*	G5	S5	P	X
Red-breasted Nuthatch	*Sitta canadensis*	G5	S4	PP	
Brown Creeper	*Certhia americana*	G5	S4	PP	
Winter Wren	*Troglodytes troglodytes*	G5	S5	PP	
Golden-crowned Kinglet	*Regulus satrapa*	G5	S4S5	PP	
Ruby-crowned Kinglet	*Regulus calendula*	G5	S5B	PP	X
Arctic Warbler	*Phylloscopus borealis*	G5	S5B		NEW
American Dipper	*Cinclus mexicanus*	G5	S5	P	X
Gray-cheeked Thrush	*Catharus minimus*	G5	S4S5B	P	X
Swainson's Thrush	*Catharus ustulatus*	G5	S5B	P	X
Hermit Thrush	*Catharus guttatus*	G5	S5B	P	X
American Robin	*Turdus migratorius*	G5	S5B	P	X
Varied Thrush	*Ixoreus naevius*	G5	S5B	P	X
Orange-crowned Warbler	*Oreothlypis celata*	G5	S5B	P	X
Yellow Warbler	*Dendroica petechia*	G5	S5B	P	X

Common Name	Scientific Name	Global Rank[1]	State Rank[1]	Previously Recorded	Recorded in 2011
Yellow-rumped Warbler	*Dendroica coronata*	G5	S5B	P	X
Blackpoll Warbler	*Dendroica striata*	G5	S4B	P	X
Northern Waterthrush	*Parkesia noveboracensis*	G5	S4S5B	P	X
Wilson's Warbler	*Wilsonia pusilla*	G5	S5B	P	X
American Tree Sparrow	*Spizella arborea*	G5	S5B	P	X
Savannah Sparrow	*Passerculus sandwichensis*	G5	S5B	P	X
Fox Sparrow	*Passerella iliaca*	G5	S5B, S3N	P	X
Song Sparrow	*Melospiza melodia*	G5	S5	PP	
Lincoln's Sparrow	*Melospiza lincolnii*	G5	S5B	PP	X
White-crowned Sparrow	*Zonotrichia leucophrys*	G5	S5B	P	X
Golden-crowned Sparrow	*Zonotrichia atricapilla*	G5	S5B	P	X
Dark-eyed Junco	*Junco hyemalis*	G5	S5B	P	X
Lapland Longspur	*Calcarius lapponicus*	G5	S5B	PP	
Snow Bunting	*Plectrophenax nivalis*	G5	S5	PP	
McKay's Bunting	*Plectrophenax hyperboreus*	G3	S3	PP	
Rusty Blackbird	*Euphagus carolinus*	G4	S4B, S3N	PP	X
Pine Grosbeak	*Pinicola enucleator*	G5	S5	PP	X
White-winged Crossbill	*Loxia leucoptera*	G5	S5	PP	X
Common Redpoll	*Acanthis flammea*	G5	S5	P	X*
Hoary Redpoll	*Acanthis hornemanni*	G5	S5	PP	X*
Pine Siskin	*Spinus pinus*	G5	S4S5	PP	X

Total species detected during inventory: 76 (Common and Hoary Redpoll combined as a single species)
Total species on Park Service List: 123

X* = Given the difficulty in distinguishing between Common and Hoary Redpolls, we recorded all redpolls as 'redpoll species'. Based on the distribution of both species, most redpolls seen along the Alagnak Wild River were likely Common Redpolls (Know and Lowther 2000a, 2000b).

[1] Definitions for Global and State Heritage Conservation Status Ranks: G/SX = Presumed extinct = Believed to be extinct throughout its range, G/SH = Possibly extinct = Known from only historical locations, but may nevertheless still be extant, G/S1 = Critically imperiled = Critically imperiled because of extreme rarity or because of some factor(s) making it especially vulnerable to extinction, G/S2 = Imperiled = Imperiled because of rarity or because of some factor(s) making it especially vulnerable to extinction, G/S3 = Vulnerable = Vulnerable either because very rare and local throughout its range, found only in a restricted range, or because of other factors making it vulnerable to extinction, G/S4 = Apparently secure = Uncommon but not rare, and usually widespread. Does not appear vulnerable in most of its range, but possibly cause for long-term concern, G/S5 = Secure = Common, widespread, and abundant. Not vulnerable in most of its range.

Table 2. Species of conservation concern recorded along the Alagnak Wild River, Alaska. Species detected during the 2011 inventory are represented with an 'X'. Species that were not recorded during the 2011 inventory, but are on the National Park bird checklist (NPSpecies 2008) are represented with a 'P' indicating Present and 'PP' indicating Probably Present.

Common Name	Conservation Status Determined by Program[1]				
	Audubon	NALCP	USFWS	ASCP	LCPA
Detected during 2011 inventory					
Willow Ptarmigan		X			
Peregrine Falcon		X	X		
Lesser Yellowlegs	X		X	X	
Whimbrel	X		X	X	
Hudsonian Godwit	X		X	X	
Bar-tailed Godwit	X		X	X	
Arctic Tern			X		
Short-eared Owl		X			
Gray-cheeked Thrush					X
Varied Thrush	X				X
Blackpoll Warbler	X				X
Golden-crowned Sparrow					X
Rusty Blackbird	X				X
Undetected during 2011 inventory, but expected					
Brant	P				
Black Scoter	PP				
Rock Ptarmigan		PP			
Red-throated Loon	PP		PP		
Rough-legged Hawk		P			
Gyrfalcon		PP			PP
American Golden-Plover	PP			PP	
Short-billed Dowitcher	P		P	P	
Olive-sided Flycatcher	P				
Lapland Longspur		PP			
Snow Bunting		PP			
McKay's Bunting	PP	PP	PP		PP
Hoary Redpoll*		PP			PP

[1] Audubon = Audubon Alaska Watchlist (Kirchoff and Padula 2010), NALCP = North American Landbird Conservation Plan (Rich et al. 2004), USFWS = U.S. Fish and Wildlife Service's Birds of Conservation Concern (U.S. Fish and Wildlife Service 2008), ASCP = Alaska Shorebird Conservation Plan (Alaska Shorebird Group 2008), LCPA = Landbird Conservation Plan for Alaska (Boreal Partners in Flight Working Group 1999).
*Potentially detected but unconfirmed.

Bird Occurrence and Relative Abundance

Frequency of occurrence summaries are based on detections made at the 9 grids where we conducted 71 point count surveys during the June breeding season. We detected 943 birds of 49 unique species in ALAG during point counts. Overall we encountered 12.11 (± 4.62 SE) individuals of 7.7 (± 2.2 SE) species per point (Table 3). The five most common species were represented by four passerines (Wilson's Warbler, American Tree Sparrow, Savannah Sparrow, White-crowned Sparrow) and one shorebird (Greater Yellowlegs).

The species with the highest average occurrence (i.e., highest mean per-point abundance) also had the highest percent detection (i.e., were recorded on the highest proportion of points). Wilson's Warbler, White-crowned Sparrow, Savannah Sparrow, and American Tree Sparrow were observed at 70.4%, 54.9%, 52.1%, and 50.7% of sites sampled, respectively. Other species included the Yellow-rumped Warbler, Orange-crowned Warbler, and Greater Yellowlegs, which were each detected at > 40% of the points.

Table 3. Occurrence of birds on 10-minute points counts during the inventory of breeding birds in Alagnak Wild River, Alaska, June 2011.

Common Name	Total Detected	Average Occurrence[1]	No. Points on Which Detected	Percent Detection[2]
Tundra Swan	14	0.197	4	5.6
American Wigeon	1	0.014	1	1.4
Common Merganser	2	0.028	2	2.8
Willow Ptarmigan	3	0.042	3	4.2
Osprey	3	0.042	1	1.4
Bald Eagle	2	0.028	2	2.8
Northern Harrier	3	0.042	3	4.2
Northern Goshawk	1	0.014	1	1.4
Sandhill Crane	15	0.211	8	11.3
Greater Yellowlegs	49	0.690	30	42.3
Lesser Yellowlegs	4	0.056	2	2.8
Whimbrel	43	0.606	17	23.9
Hudsonian Godwit	19	0.268	7	9.9
Wilson's Snipe	35	0.493	20	28.2
Bonaparte's Gull	3	0.042	2	2.8
Mew Gull	13	0.183	6	8.5
Glaucous-winged Gull	15	0.211	6	8.5
Arctic Tern	15	0.211	10	14.1
Downy Woodpecker	2	0.028	2	2.8
Alder Flycatcher	10	0.141	7	9.9
Gray Jay	27	0.380	24	33.8
Black-billed Magpie	2	0.028	2	2.8
Common Raven	4	0.056	3	4.2
Tree Swallow	1	0.014	1	1.4
Black-capped Chickadee	4	0.056	3	4.2
Boreal Chickadee	5	0.070	4	5.6
Ruby-crowned Kinglet	2	0.028	2	2.8
Gray-cheeked Thrush	6	0.085	6	8.5

Common Name	Total Detected	Average Occurrence[1]	No. Points on Which Detected	Percent Detection[2]
Swainson's Thrush	3	0.042	3	4.2
Hermit Thrush	41	0.577	23	32.4
American Robin	5	0.070	5	7.0
Varied Thrush	6	0.085	3	4.2
Orange-crowned Warbler	39	0.549	30	42.3
Yellow Warbler	3	0.042	2	2.8
Yellow-rumped Warbler	43	0.606	31	43.7
Blackpoll Warbler	37	0.521	28	39.4
Northern Waterthrush	46	0.648	22	31.0
Wilson's Warbler	99	1.394	50	70.4
American Tree Sparrow	76	1.070	36	50.7
Savannah Sparrow	70	0.986	37	52.1
Fox Sparrow	20	0.282	16	22.5
Lincoln's Sparrow	10	0.141	9	12.7
White-crowned Sparrow	57	0.803	39	54.9
Golden-crowned Sparrow	16	0.225	11	15.5
Dark-eyed Junco	12	0.169	7	9.9
Rusty Blackbird	1	0.014	1	1.4
White-winged Crossbill	41	0.577	9	12.7
Redpoll species	14	0.197	10	14.1
Pine Siskin	1	0.014	1	1.4
Total number of Individuals:	943	12.11 ± 4.62 SE		
Total number of Species:	49	7.7 ± 2.2 SE		
Total number of Points:	71			

[1]Average Occurrence = number of individuals detected/number of points surveyed
[2]% Detection = (number of points on which detected/number of points surveyed) x 100

Species Distribution

Summaries of species distribution are based on all observations collected during visits to the 9 survey grids as well as incidental species recorded during four travel days along the river corridor, for a total of 13 possible detection "grids". Grid by grid species occurrences are presented in Appendix 4. The distribution of species across the 13 grids was similar to their frequency of occurrence (Table 3), in that commonly detected species were typically widely distributed and infrequently detected species had more restricted distributions. For instance, eight species were detected in 10 or more grids. These included the five species with the highest number of detections (Wilson's Warbler, American Tree Sparrow, Savannah Sparrow, White-crowned Sparrow, and Greater Yellowlegs), as well as Arctic Tern, Orange-crowned Warbler, and Northern Waterthrush. Eighteen species were only detected within a single grid, and were usually only represented by a single detection (Table 3, Appendix 4).

16

Elevational Distribution of Surveys and Habitats

Due to the limited elevational gradient along the Alagnak River (10 m to 300 m), our survey was not stratified by elevation. Here, we include some general observations about elevational differences and habitats observed along the river, but they were not used in any bird habitat association analyses.

We conducted 32 (45%) point count surveys at low elevations (<100 m), 20 (28%) at middle elevations (100-200 m), and 19 (27%) at high elevations (>200 m). Elevation was highest (250-300 m) along the upper river and gradually decreased to around 10 m at the lower ALAG boundary. Just over half of the river was categorized as low elevation and about a quarter was categorized as each high and middle elevation. Point counts at low elevations were primarily in low shrub and needleleaf forest habitats, at middle elevations in dwarf and low shrub, and at high elevations in needleleaf forest, mixed and broadleaf forest, and dwarf shrub.

Bird-Habitat Associations

To assess patterns of bird habitat use, we summarized the percent cover of the five simplified habitat types at survey points at which the 8 most commonly detected species (> 10 detections) were recorded (Figure 3). Overall, low and dwarf shrub was the most common habitat type encountered at survey points, detected at 38% of all points and comprised the greatest average percent cover (38%). Herbaceous habitats were the least common habitat encountered, present at just 8% of all points, and comprised an average of 6% total cover.

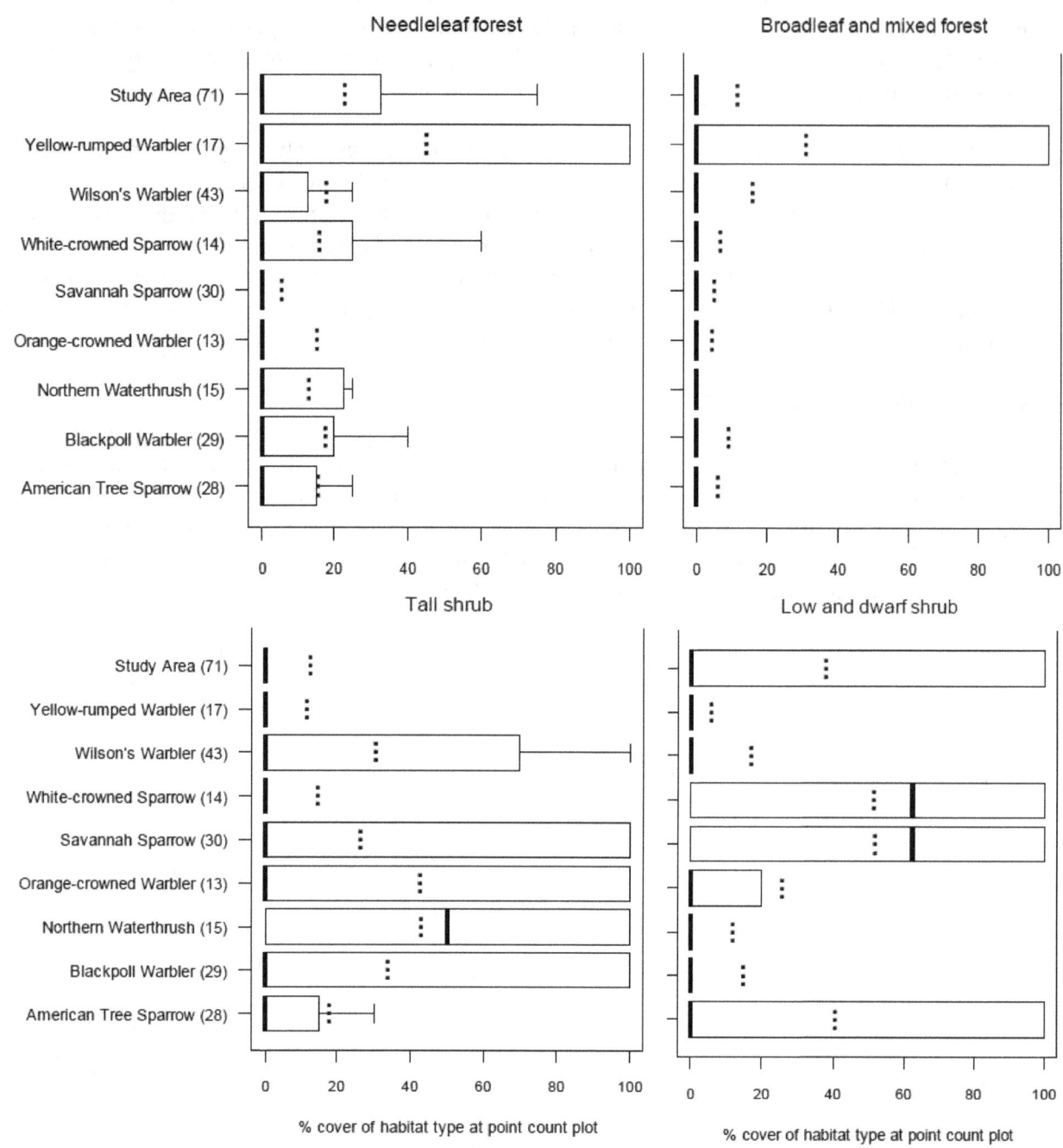

Figure 3. Percent cover of most common habitats types at point count locations for the most common bird species, Alagnak Wild River, Alaska, June 2011. Box plots show median (thin vertical line), mean (vertical dotted line), quartiles (boxes), and 1.5 times the interquartile range (whiskers). Number of detections is shown in parentheses for each species.

Needleleaf Forest

Forest habitat was divided into two categories: needleleaf and broadleaf and mixed. Needleleaf forest was comprised of white and/or black spruce trees (*Picea mariana* and *P. glauca*). Needleleaf forest was recorded at twenty-one (30%) of the points, and included habitats with greater than 10% needleleaf trees (> 3 m tall). The majority (90%) of needleleaf forest points were classified as either open forest (25-65% needleleaf cover) or woodland (10-25% needleleaf cover), indicating the canopy was relatively open, allowing shrubs and herbaceous plants to grow in the understory (Figure 4). Yellow-rumped Warblers were common at points (45% cover ± 12.1 SE) in needleleaf forest and woodland habitats. Other species with moderate associations to needleleaf habitats included Wilson's Warbler (18% cover ± 5.3 SE), Blackpoll Warbler (18% cover ± 6.0 SE), White-crowned Sparrow (16% cover ± 8.2 SE), American Tree Sparrow (16% cover ± 6.1 SE), and Orange-crowned Warbler (15% cover ± 10.4 SE) (Figure 3).

Broadleaf and Mixed Forest

The other dominant forest type, broadleaf and mixed forest, was detected at 17% (n = 12) of survey points and included habitats with greater than 10% broadleaf and/or needleleaf trees (> 3 meters tall). Most (75%) of the broadleaf and mixed forest points were classified as either open forest (25-60% tree cover) or woodland (10-25%) tree cover with open canopies and shrubs in the understory. Broadleaf forest was characterized by paper birch (*Betula neoalaskana*) and mixed forest was characterized by paper birch (*B. neoalaskana*) and spruce (*P. mariana* and/or *P. glauca*) (Figure 5). Similar to results from needlefeaf forest, Yellow-rumped Warblers also showed a strong association for this forest type (present at points with a mean of 31% [± 11.2 SE] cover) and Wilson's Warblers demonstrated a moderate association (present at points with a mean of 16% [± 5.1 SE] cover) (Figure 3).

Tall Shrub

Ten (14%) of the survey points were classified as containing tall shrubs between 1.5 and 3 meters in height. Tall shrub habitat was dominated by willow (*Salix* spp.) and alder (*Alnus incana* spp. *tenuifola*) (Figure 6). Birds commonly at points with a higher percent cover of the tall shrub habitat were Northern Waterthrush (43% cover ± 11.8 SE), Orange-crowned Warbler (43% cover ± 13.6 SE), Blackpoll Warbler (43% cover ± 8.3 SE), Wilson's Warbler (31% cover ± 6.5 SE), and Savannah Sparrow (27% cover ± 8.2 SE).

Low and Dwarf Shrub

Low and dwarf shrub was the most expansive habitat type throughout the study area (Figure 3). Twenty-nine (41%) survey points were classified as containing low and dwarf shrub habitat types. These contained less than 10% trees and greater than 25% low and dwarf shrubs. Low and dwarf shrub habitats were dominated by dwarf birch (*Betula nana*), crowberry (*Empetrum nigrum*), blueberry (*Vaccinium uliginosum*), cranberry (*Vaccinium vitis-idaea*), and Labrador tea (*Ledum* sp.) (Figure 7). Species commonly found at points with at least 40% low and dwarf shrub cover were White-crowned Sparrow (52% cover ± 13.1 SE), Savannah Sparrow (52% cover ± 8.9 SE), and American Tree Sparrow (40% cover ± 9.1 SE).

Herbaceous

Herbaceous habitat was limited in extent, with only 6 points (8%) falling into this habitat category. This habitat type had less than 25% woody plant cover and was characterized by graminoids, forbs, and mosses (Figure 8). The small sample size made bird-habitat associations difficult to determine, with most species not demonstrating a strong association with herbaceous habitats. Thus the herbaceous cover type was not included in the bird-habitat comparison in figure 3.

Figure 4. Open needleleaf forest consisting primarily of *Picea spp.* (spruce) and *Empetrum nigrum* (crowberry), *Betula nana* (dwarf birch), *Ledum sp.* (Labrador tea), *Vaccinium vitis-idaea* (cranberry), mosses, and lichens in the understory. Photo taken at grid 4, point 3, 3 June 2011.

Figure 5. Open mixed forest habitat consisting primarily of *Betula neoalaskana* (paper birch), *Picea glauca* (white spruce) and *Alnus sp.* (alder), *Spirea sp., Betula nana* (dwarf birch), *Vaccinium uliginosum* (blueberry), and *Calamagrostis sp.* in the understory. Photo taken at grid 4, point 9, looking downslope towards the Alagnak River, 3 June 2011.

Figure 6. Closed tall shrub habitat consisting primarily of *Salix spp.* (willow), with graminoids, mosses, and lichen in the understory. Photo taken at grid 4, point 7, 4 June 2011.

Figure 7. Low shrub habitat consisting primarily of *Ledum sp.* (Labrador tea), *Salix spp.* (willow), *Betula nana* (dwarf birch), *Vaccinum vitis-idaea* (cranberry), gaminoids, and mosses at grid 29, point 5. Photo taken 13 June 2011 near the lower Alagnak River park boundary.

Figure 8. Herbaceous habitat dominated by graminoids along the river corridor at grid 21, point 5, 10 June 2011.

Other Habitat Types

Bare ground was a unique habitat feature that was only encountered at high elevation sites along the upper section of river (Figure 9). We include it here as an example of a rare habitat type for the region. Bare ground was comprised of dwarf shrubs, graminoids, mosses, lichens, and rocks.

Figure 9. Bare ground, rocky habitat at high elevation site (317 m) in upper Alagnak River grid 3, point 11, 4 June 2011.

Discussion

This survey serves as a basic avifaunal inventory of riparian and adjacent habitat types along the Alagnak River corridor. This inventory is the first systematic ground survey of birds in the area and the last of the five SWAN park units to receive an avian inventory (Van Hemert et al. 2006, Ruthrauff et al. 2007, Ruthrauff and Tibbitts 2009). Each of SWAN park inventories has contributed to our knowledge of the distribution, abundance, and habitat use of birds in southwestern and southcentral Alaska. We hope that the results of this survey will be used to help guide monitoring, research and management decisions regarding avian fauna along the ALAG corridor as well as in adjacent areas.

Avian Detection, Distribution and Abundance

The primary goal of this inventory was to validate the existing ALAG bird checklist by documenting as many species as possible during the breeding season. Prior to this inventory, 123 avian species were listed as either present (previously documented on the river) or probably present (suspected to occur but not previously documented) within the ALAG boundary (NPSpecies 2008), of which we detected 59% (n = 73). Of those species considered present, we detected 84% (n = 61). Fourteen species listed as probably present were detected during surveys. These species, upon review, may warrant status changes to "present" in NPSpecies based on our recent confirmed observations.

Although we sampled a variety of habitat types, 35 additional species classified as probably present were not detected. Species listed as probably present but not observed included passerines that are known breeders elsewhere on the Alaska Peninsula (e.g., Northern Shrike, Song Sparrow, Snow Bunting), as well as waterfowl and shorebird species that likely occur in the region during late spring/early summer as migrants (e.g., Greater White-fronted Goose, Black Scoter, Bufflehead, and Pacific Golden-Plover). Other species categorized as probably present are generally considered rare in region (e.g., Ruddy Turnstone, Least Sandpiper, Rough-legged Hawk), and therefore, less likely to be detected. Conducting this point count inventory during the period of peak breeding was an effort to maximize our ability to detect breeding landbirds, which we feel we did successfully, but our timing and sampling method reduced our likelihood of encountering migrants and non-landbird species.

We detected three avian species during this inventory that were not previously listed as occurring in ALAG (NPSpecies 2008). The new species, American Kestrel, Bar-tailed Godwit, and Arctic Warbler, were all detected while walking between survey points. These detections highlight the importance of maintaining a checklist of birds encountered while not conducting timed surveys and the need to incorporate other survey methods to detect species poorly detected with point count methodologies. In comparison, intensive survey effort in KATM and LACL, yielded three and two new detections for the two parks, respectively (Ruthrauff et al. 2007). Each of the species has been reported elsewhere on the Alaska Peninsula, and our recent confirmed observations can be used to help delineate their ranges more clearly. The American Kestrel is listed as present in neighboring KATM and LACL, although it was not detected during surveys by Ruthrauff et al. (2007). The American Kestrel was only observed once, while in flight, thus, it remains uncertain whether the species breeds along the Alagnak River. The Bar-tailed Godwit is listed as present in LACL and the Arctic Warbler in KATM, but again, neither was detected during the 2007 inventory (Ruthrauff et al. 2007). Similar to the American Kestrel, the Bar-tailed

Godwit was only observed one time, perched in the top of a spruce tree, thus breeding status remains uncertain. The Arctic Warbler, a documented breeder in nearby King Salmon Creek (Savage 2008) and Brooks Camp was observed singing along the upper river, and therefore, potentially breeds in the area.

Our categorization of species of concern from the ALAG bird checklist includes 26 species, of which 13 were detected during this inventory. In general, species of conservation concern were neither commonly detected nor widely distributed along the Alagnak River, with the exception of the Arctic Tern, Blackpoll Warbler and Golden-crowned Sparrow. Whimbrels and Hudsonian Godwits were locally abundant in restricted areas. Ruthrauff et al. (2007) detected Whimbrels in LACL and KATM, and Hudsonian Godwits in KATM. The overall breeding distribution of the two species is poorly understood and neither has been confirmed previously breeding in the area (Skeel and Mallory 1996, Walker et al. 2011). Both species were extremely vocal and appeared to be defending territories, suggestive of breeding behavior. Locations where these species were sighted should be more intensely investigated to determine their importance to the reproduction of the species.

The ALAG checklist is essentially a subset of the KATM checklist, with 120 species in common. Such a large overlap is not surprising given the close proximity of the parks. ALAG is much smaller in areal extent than KATM, with less varied geography (lacking coastline or mountains), and fewer habitat types. Consequently, we expected to encounter fewer avian species than reported by Ruthrauff et al. (2007) during their inventory of montane nesting birds in KATM.

Ruthrauff et al. (2007) detected 92 species in KATM, while we detected 76 species on the Alagnak River. Sixty species were recorded in both parks. Sixteen species were unique to the ALAG inventory, of which 15 were expected to occur in KATM, but were not documented. There was some overlap of the most commonly detected species between the two survey areas (e.g., Wilson's Warbler, American Tree Sparrow), while higher elevation species were more common in KATM (e.g., Golden-crowned Sparrow, American Pipit), and several lower elevation species considered common along the Alagnak River were only rarely detected in the KATM survey (e.g., Blackpoll Warbler, Northern Waterthrush). The KATM surveys focused on middle and high elevation habitats, with all surveys conducted above 100 m, while the ALAG surveys were generally between 10 and 332 m and adjacent to riparian buffers, which could account for these differences. Detection rates were lower in KATM, averaging 6.42 (± 0.21 SE) individuals of 4.03 (± 0.12 SE) species per point, compared to detection rates of 12.11 (± 4.62 SE) individuals of 7.7 (± 2.2 SE) species per point in ALAG. The lower detection rates in KATM were likely a reflection of survey design, since fewer birds are typically detected at higher elevation plots (Ruthrauff et al. 2007).

Patterns of Habitat Use

Along the Alagnak River corridor, forests typically occupied the lower elevation sites, giving way to tall and low shrub habitats at middle elevation sites, with dwarf shrub and herbaceous vegetation most common at the highest sites. Compared to neighboring KATM, ANIA and LACL, the elevational gradient along the Alagnak River and adjacent areas surveyed was moderate. In other SWAN parks, habitat types and the bird communities they supported varied with elevation (ranging from 100 to 1,620 m) (Ruthrauff et al. 2007, Ruthrauff and Tibbitts 2009). Landscape features in ALAG did not include high mountain peaks, steep topography, or coastal areas that would contribute to such a wide range of elevations, thus we did not conduct elevation association type analyzes.

In general, bird species were most strongly associated with shrub habitats. Wilson's Warbler, Orange-crowned Warbler, Northern Waterthrush, Blackpoll Warbler, and Savannah Sparrow were all associated with survey sites with > 20% tall shrub cover. White-crowned Sparrow, Savannah Sparrow, and American Tree Sparrow were all associated with > 40% low and dwarf shrub. These associations were expected based on published habitat preferences of the species (Pogson et al. 1997, Kessel 1998, Cotter and Andres 2000) and similar species-specific patterns of habitat use in other SWAN parks (Ruthrauff et al. 2007, Ruthrauff and Tibbitts 2009). Yellow-rumped Warbler, a species often found in forest habitats (Noon et al. 1980, Sabo 1980, Douglas et al. 1992), was associated with both needleleaf and broadleaf/mixed forest habitats.

Species commonly associated with shrubs (Wilson's Warbler, Orange-crowned Warbler, Northern Waterthrush, Blackpoll Warbler, Savannah Sparrow, White-crowned Sparrow, and American-Tree Sparrow) were also associated with needleleaf forest habitats in this inventory. These needleleaf habitats were often a mosaic of habitat types with a relatively low percent cover of needleleaf trees. Thus, the needleleaf habitat likely contained shrubs in the forest and in the surrounding habitats. Strong bird associations were not found in the broadleaf/mixed forest habitats, likely due to the Viereck system classifying open forest and woodland habitats within the broader forest type, although they contained a large percentage of understory vegetation (i.e., shrubs) that is important to birds. Very few points were sampled in the herbaceous habitat type, making it difficult to associate species with herbaceous vegetation.

Recommendations for Future Study

This inventory enhances our understanding of the status and distribution of breeding birds in ALAG. To manage landscapes for optimal bird conservation, land managers need a site-level understanding of bird distribution and abundance (Sullivan et al. 2009). We acknowledge that our survey was far from complete. We only detected birds present during a two week window during the early breeding season. Although this period likely encompassed the time of greatest avian abundance and diversity, accurate information on the occurrence and distribution of birds during other seasons of the year is generally lacking. Recording the occurrence of species using the Alagnak River during the non-breeding season (i.e. during migration and residents during the non-breeding season) would more accurately document the parks avian resources.

Additionally, in order to be consistent with all other SWAN breeding bird inventories, our surveys used point count methodologies. Although point count surveys are widely used, they have limitations for estimating abundance and trends (Buckland et al. 2001, Buckland 2006). Since the primary goal of our survey was to compile a baseline avian species list, we did not use advanced analytical techniques (i.e., distance estimation) to calculate detectability and corrected abundance. We would recommend recording distances and modeling detection probability in future surveys, as it is vital for enabling more complete and statistically valid comparisons to be made between and within species and across different habitats. Furthermore, we recommend using additional survey techniques (i.e., line transect for birds that flush easily, area searches for more secretive species, etc.) to inventory for species that are not well detected on point count surveys in order to acquire an adequate sample size for other groups of avian species (Buckland et al. 2001).

We surveyed fewer plots than we had originally planned because of the amount of time it took to move camp and float the river corridor. More time would be needed to increase the number of grids sampled, which would in turn increase the number of points in each habitat type and improve bird habitat association analyses. Areas of particular interest where we recommend additional sampling effort include high and middle elevation areas, which only occur along the upper reaches of the river. Due to time restrictions, we were only able to sample two high and two middle elevation grids. High elevation grids contain unique habitats above spruce-line, with bare ground and dwarf shrub/ lichen that is not found elsewhere on the river, and may harbor a different bird community (Figure 10). Other potentially unique habitats we were unable to sample included isolated stands of dense birch-cottonwood forest and freshwater aquatic bed habitats that may be important for waterfowl.

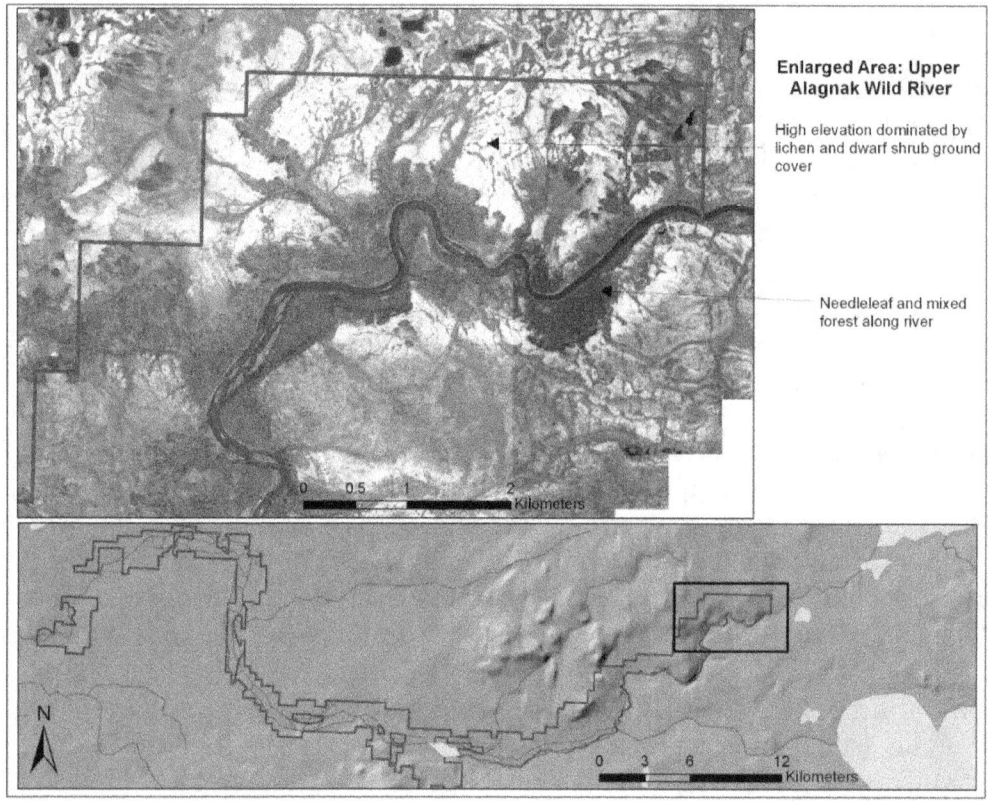

Figure 10. Upland area of interest in to spend more time in during future bird surveys along the upper Alagnak Wild River, Alask

Conclusions

Information on breeding birds gathered during this inventory can be used as a baseline to help researchers and resource managers plan studies that will assess anthropogenic impacts, climate change impacts, and assist with future management decisions. Similar methodologies employed across Alaska provide a consistent foundation upon which to direct future monitoring (Arctic Network- Tibbitts et al. 2005; Yukon-Charley Rivers National Preserve- Swanson and Nigro 2003; Kenai Fjords NPP- Van Hemert et al. 2006, KATM and LACL - Ruthrauff et al. 2007; ANIA- Ruthrauff and Tibbitts 2009). All southwest Alaska network parks now have received a baseline inventory of avian species, which provides a solid foundation for the NPS inventory and monitoring program to work from. With the increased knowledge provided by these studies, managers can better promote the conservation and appreciation of birds both within and beyond park boundaries.

Literature Cited

Alaska Shorebird Group. 2008. A Conservation plan for Alaska shorebirds. Unpublished report. Alaska Shorebird Working Group. Available through U.S. Fish and Wildlife Service, Migratory Bird Management, Anchorage, Alaska. 47 pp.

Boreal Partners in Flight Working Group. 1999. Landbird conservation plan for Alaska biogeographic regions. Version 1.0. Unpubl. Rep., U. S. Fish and Wildlife Service, Anchorage, Alaska. 45pp.

Buckland, S. T. 2006. Point transect surveys for songbirds: robust methodologies. The Auk 123: 345-357.

Buckland, S. T., D. R. Anderson, K. P. Burnham, J. L. Laake, D. L. Borchers, and L. Thomas. 2001. Introduction to distance sampling. Oxford University Press, New York. 432 pp.

Cotter, P. A. and B. A. Andres. 2000. Breeding bird habitat associations on the Alaska Breeding Bird Survey: USGS, Biological Resources Division Information and Technology Report USGS/BRD/ITR-2000-0010, 53 p.

Douglas, D. C., J. T. Ratti, R. A. Black, and J. R. Alldredge. 1992. Avian habitat associations in riparian zones of Idaho's Centennial Mountains. Wilson Bulletin 104:485-500.

Handel, C. M. and M. N. Cady. 2004. Alaska landbird monitoring survey: Protocol for setting up and conducting point count surveys. Sponsored by Boreal Partners in Flight, Unpublished protocol. USGS Alaska Science Center, Anchorage, Alaska. 46 pp.

Kessel, B. 1998. Habitat characteristics of some passerine birds in western North American taiga. University of Alaska Press, Fairbanks, Alaska. 117 p.

Kirchoff, M. D. and V. Padula. 2010. Alaska Watchlist 2010. Audubon Alaska, Anchorage, Alaska. 8 pp.

Knox, A. G. and P. E. Lowther. 2000a. Common Redpoll (*Carduelis flammea*). The Birds of North America Online (A. Poole, Ed.). Cornell Lab of Ornithology, Ithaca, NY. Retrieved from Birds of North America Online: http://bna.birds.cornell.edu/bna/species/543. (accessed 9 January 2012).

Knox, A. G. and P. E. Lowther. 2000b. Hoary Redpoll (*Carduelis hornemanni*). The Birds of North America Online (A. Poole, Ed.). Cornell Lab of Ornithology, Ithaca, NY. Retrieved from Birds of North America Online: http://bna.birds.cornell.edu/bna/species/544. (accessed 9 January 2012).

LANDFIRE: LANDFIRE 1.0.0. Existing vegetation type layer. U.S. Department of Interior, Geological Survey.

Lenz, J., T. Gotthardt, M. Kelly, and R. Lipkin. 2001. Final Report: compilation of existing species data in Alaska's National Parks. Prepared for the National Park Service Inventory and Monitoring Program. Alaska Natural Heritage Program, University of Alaska Anchorage. 127 pp.

MacDonald, S. O. and J. A. Cook. 2009. Recent mammals of Alaska. University of Alaska Press, Fairbanks, Alaska.

MacKenzie, D. I. 2005. What are the issues of presence-absence data for wildlife managers? Journal of Wildlife Management 69:849-860.

McCullogh, B., W. Hobbins, and W. Hill.1997. Alagnak Wild River 1997 park report – flora and fauna observations. Unpublished field notes.

National Park Service (NPS). 2003. Land cover map of Katmai National Park and Preserve-2000. Alaska Natural Heritage Program. Geospatial Dataset-1040876.

National Park Service (NPS). 2006. National Park Service Alaska region science strategy. Available online: http://planning.nps.gov/document/NPS_strategic_plan.pdf. (accessed 17 January 2012).

National Park Service (NPS). 2011. Alagnak Wild River. National Park Service, U. S. Department of the Interior. Available from http://www.nps.gov/alag/ (accessed 17 January 2012).

Noon, B. R., D. K. Dawson, D. B. Inkly, C. S. Robbins, and S. H. Anderson. 1980. Consistency in habitat preference of forest bird species. Transactions North American Wildlife Natural Resources Conference 45:226-244.

NPSpecies. 2008. Certified organisms. The National Park Service species database. Available from https://irma.nps.gov/App/Species/Welcome (accessed 12 January 2012).

Pogson, T. H., S. E. Quinlan, and B. Lehnhausen. 1997. A manual of selected neotropical migrant birds of Alaska national forests. USDA, USFS, Juneau, Alaska.

Rich, T.D., C.J. Beardmore, H. Berlanga, P.J. Blancher, M.S.W. Bradstreet, G.S. Butcher, D.W. Demarest, E.H. Dunn, W.C. Hunter, E.E. Inigo-Elias, J.A. Kennedy, A.M. Martell, A.O. Panjabi, D.N. Pashley, K.V. Rosenberg, C.M. Rustay, J.S. Wendt, and T.C. Will. 2004. Partners in Flight North American landbird conservation plan. Cornell Lab of Ornithology, Ithaca, New York.

Royle, J. A., D. K. Dawson, and S. Bates, 2004. Modeling abundance effects in distance sampling. Ecology 85:1591-1597.

Ruthrauff, D. R., and T. L. Tibbitts. 2009. Inventory of breeding birds in Aniakchak National Monument and Preserve. Unpublished final report for National Park Service. U.S. Geological Survey, Alaska Science Center, Anchorage, Alaska.

Ruthrauff, D. R., T. L. Tibbitts, R. E. Gill, Jr., and C. M. Handel. 2007. Inventory of montane-nesting birds in Katmai and Lake Clark National Parks and Preserves. Unpublished final report for National Park Service. U. S. Geological Survey, Alaska Science Center, Anchorage, Alaska.

Sabo, S. R. 1980. Niche and habitat relations in subalpine bird communities of the White Mountains of New Hampshire, U.S.A. Ecological Monographs 50:241-60.

Savage, S. 1997. Bird observations: Alagnak Wild River. Katmai National Park and Preserve, King Salmon, Alaska.

Savage, S. 2008. Personal Communication with Tamara Fields regarding KATM and ANIA sightings. U. S. Fish and Wildlife Service, King Salmon, AK.

Skeel, M. A., and E. P. Mallory. 1996. Whimbrel (*Numenius phaeopus*). The Birds of North America Online (A. Poole, Ed.). Cornell Lab of Ornithology, Ithaca, NY. Retrieved from Birds of North America Online: http://bna.birds.cornell.edu/bna/species/219. (accessed 23 January 2012).

Sullivan, B. L., C. L. Wood, M. J. Iliff, R. E. Bonney, D. Fink, and S. Kelling. 2009. eBird: A citizen-based observation network in the biological sciences. Biological Conservation 142: 2282-2292.

Swanson, S. A. and D. A. Nigro. 2003. A breeding landbird inventory of Yukon-Charley Rivers National Preserve, Alaska, June 1999 and 2000. Unpubl. Report YUCH-03-001, National Park Service, Fairbanks, Alaska.

Tibbitts, T. L., D. R. Ruthrauff, R. E. Gill, Jr., and C. M. Handel. 2005. Inventory of montane-nesting birds in the Arctic Network of National Parks, Alaska. Arctic Network Inventory and Monitoring Program, National Park Service, NPS/AKARCN/NRTR-2006/02, Fairbanks, Alaska.

Tyre, A. J., B. Tenhumberg, S. A. Field, D. Niejalke, K. Parris, and H. P. Possingham. 2003. Improving precision and reducing bias in biological surveys: estimating false-negative error rates. Ecological Applications 13:1790–1801.

U.S. Fish and Wildlife Service. 2008. Birds of conservation concern 2008. Division of Migratory Bird Management, Arlington, Virginia.

Van Hemert, C., C. M. Handel, M. N. Cady, and J. Terenzi. 2006. Summer inventory of landbirds in Kenai Fjords National Park. Unpublished final report for National Park Service. U. S. Geological Survey, Alaska Science Center, Anchorage, Alaska.

Viereck, L. A., C. T. Dryness, A. R. Batten, and K. J. Wenzlick. 1992. The Alaska vegetation classification. Gen. Tech. Rep. PNW-GTR-286.

Walker. B. M., N. R. Senner, C. S. Elphick, and J. Kilma. 2011. Hudsonian Godwit (*Limosa haemastica*). The Birds of North America Online (A. Poole, Ed.). Cornell Lab of Ornithology, Ithaca, NY. Retrieved from Birds of North America Online: http://bna.birds.cornell.edu/bna/species/629. (accessed 23 January 2012).

Appendix 1: Sample Stratification

Allocation of sample points by land cover type for the Alagnak Wild River avian inventory, 2011. Land cover types are divided by upper and lower river, since each section utilized a different land cover basemap.

Land cover type	Total area within sampling frame (km^2)	Number of points allocated	Number of points surveyed
Upper Alagnak- Katmai Land Cover Map			
Birch Forest	3.31	6	1
Closed Spruce Forest	0.03	1	0
Cottonwood/Poplar Forest	0.57	1	0
Dwarf Shrub	15.85	43	6
Dwarf Shrub/Bryophyte	0.15	2	1
Dwarf Shrub/Mesic Herbaceous	16.28	35	6
Lichen	0.61	3	0
Low Willow Shrub	6.02	13	1
Mesic Herbaceous	3.49	11	2
Mixed Deciduous/Conifer Forest	1.31	6	1
Mixed Low/Dwarf Shrub	7.60	18	5
Open Spruce Forest	4.74	19	4
Spruce Woodland	6.44	12	3
Tall Alder Shrub	3.24	11	4
Tall Willow Shrub	2.37	5	2
Water	3.67	3	0
Wet Herbaceous	4.54	8	3
Lower Alagnak- LANDFIRE Map			
Balsam Poplar-Aspen Woodland	0.37	4	1
Birch-Aspen Forest	0.30	1	1
Black Spruce Forest and Woodland	0.04	2	1
Dwarf Shrubland	5.69	19	7
Floodplain Forest and Shrubland	0.84	1	0
Freshwater Marsh	2.13	4	2
Herbaceous Meadow	0.64	2	0
Open Water	3.50	3	2
Shrub and Herbaceous Peatlands	10.16	28	4
Spruce-Lichen Woodland	0.22	4	2
Tussock Tundra	1.26	10	2
White Spruce Forest and Woodland	0.32	1	1
White Spruce-Hardwood Forest and Woodland	6.46	13	6
Willow Shrubland	1.25	6	3
Total	113.41	295	71

Appendix 2: Viereck Classification System

Vegetation classification (Viereck et al. 1992) used during the inventory of breeding birds in Alagnak Wild River, 2011.

Level I	Level II	Level III
I. Forest	A. Needleleaf (conifer) forest	1. Closed needleleaf forest 2. Open needleleaf forest 3. Needleleaf woodland
	B. Broadleaf forest	1. Closed broadleaf forest 2. Open broadleaf forest 3. Broadleaf woodland
	C. Mixed forest	1. Closed mixed forest 2. Open mixed forest 3. Mixed woodland
II. Scrub	A. Dwarf tree scrub	1. Closed dwarf tree scrub 2. Open dwarf tree scrub 3. Dwarf tree scrub woodland
	B. Tall scrub	1. Closed tall scrub 2. Open tall scrub
	C. Low scrub	1. Closed low scrub 2. Open low scrub
	D. Dwarf scrub	1. Dryas dwarf scrub 2. Ericaceous dwarf scrub 3. Willow dwarf scrub
III. Herbaceous	A. Graminoid herbaceous	1. Dry graminoid herbaceous 2. Mesic graminoid herbaceous 3. Wet graminoid herbaceous
	B. Forb herbaceous	1. Dry forb herbaceous 2. Mesic forb herbaceous 3. Wet forb herbaceous
	C. Bryoid herbaceous	1. Bryophyte (mosses) 2. Lichens
	D. Aquatic herbaceous	1. Freshwater aquatic herbaceous 2. Brackish water aquatic herbaceous 3. Marine aquatic herbaceous
IV. Non vegetated	*A. Water*	*1. Creek, river, lake, pond*
	B. Rock	*2. Scree, boulders, rocky ground*

Italicized categories were added to the classification to accommodate specific situations encountered during the inventory.

Appendix 3: Annotated List of Amphibian and Mammal Records

Annotated list of mammals and amphibians recorded during the inventory of breeding birds along the Alagnak River, 2011. Common and scientific names follow MacDonald and Cook (2009).

Amphibian

Wood frog (*Lithobates sylvaticus*): A wood frog was heard calling in a small high elevation (~317 m) pond near grid 3, point 11.

Mammals

Arctic ground squirrel (*Spermophilus parryii*): Sign of arctic ground squirrels were seen in grid 4.

Red squirrel (*Tamiasciurus hudsonicus*): Red squirrels were seen on grids 11, 12, and 21.

Beaver (*Castor canadensis*): A beaver was seen in grid 14 and dams, lodges, and sign of browse were seen along the river corridor.

Porcupine (*Erethizon dorsatum*): A porcupine was seen in grids 12 and 30, both walking on the ground in woodland areas.

Wolf (*Canis lupis*): Evidence of wolves was seen in the form of scat and tracks in grids 14, 21, and 29.

Coyote (*Canis latrens*): Sign of coyotes were seen in grid 12.

Red fox (*Vulpes vulpes*): A red fox was observed on grid 29 and sign was seen on grids 12 and 14.

Brown bear (*Ursus arctos*): Evidence of brown bears was found in most grids in the form of scat, tracks, and at one camp a vocalization.

River otter (*Lontra canadensis*): One river otter was seen swimming in the Alagnak River between the last grid (30) and the take out location.

Moose (*Alces americanus*): Moose were seen on three grids (3, 4, and 14) and scat and sign of browse was seen in most grids. On grid 21, we found a leg from a moose calf, indicating a recent bear kill.

Caribou (*Rangifer tarandus*): Evidence of caribou was seen in the form of scat and sheds (antlers) in grids 4 and 21.

Appendix 4: Species Occurrence by Grid

Avian species occurrence by grid or river day number (assigned to days between grids when observations were recorded).

Common Name	Grid Number									River Day Number				Number of Detections
	3	4	11	12	21	23	24	29	30	R1	R2	R3	R4	
Tundra Swan				X	X			X	X					4
American Wigeon				X				X	X	X			X	5
Mallard				X				X	X	X		X		5
Northern Shoveler								X	X				X	3
Green-winged Teal								X				X		2
Greater Scaup								X						1
Harlequin Duck												X		1
Long-tailed Duck										X				1
Common Goldeneye								X						1
Barrow's Goldeneye				X						X				2
Common Merganser				X	X							X	X	4
Red-breasted Merganser				X										1
Spruce Grouse	X													1
Willow Ptarmigan	X	X												2
Common Loon				X										1
Osprey						X		X			X		X	4
Bald Eagle	X	X						X		X		X		5
Northern Harrier	X	X	X	X				X	X				X	7
Northern Goshawk									X					1
Merlin		X		X							X			3
American Kestrel	X	X												2
Peregrine Falcon											X			1
Sandhill Crane			X	X	X			X	X	X			X	7
Semipalmated Plover									X				X	2
Spotted Sandpiper												X		1
Greater Yellowlegs	X	X	X	X	X		X	X	X	X		X		10
Lesser Yellowlegs	X							X	X		X		X	5
Whimbrel			X	X										2
Hudsonian Godwit								X	X					2
Bar-tailed Godwit										X				1
Wilson's Snipe	X	X	X	X	X			X	X					7
Bonaparte's Gull				X						X	X	X	X	5
Mew Gull	X	X	X		X					X				5
Glaucous-winged Gull								X	X					2

Common Name	Grid Number									River Day Number				Number of Detections
	3	4	11	12	21	23	24	29	30	R1	R2	R3	R4	
Arctic Tern	X	X	X	X	X	X	X			X		X	X	10
Northern Hawk Owl				X										1
Short-eared Owl								X	X					2
Boreal Owl				X										1
Belted Kingfisher												X		1
Downy Woodpecker				X					X					2
Hairy Woodpecker					X									1
American Three-toed Woodpecker	X		X											2
Alder Flycatcher			X	X	X							X		4
Gray Jay	X	X	X	X	X			X	X			X		8
Black-billed Magpie	X	X						X	X	X		X		5
Common Raven	X	X	X		X							X		5
Tree Swallow				X	X								X	3
Bank Swallow													X	1
Black-capped Chickadee		X	X	X	X									4
Boreal Chickadee	X		X	X				X						4
Arctic Warbler	X													1
Ruby-crowned Kinglet	X	X	X											3
American Dipper											X			1
Gray-cheeked Thrush	X	X	X		X							X	X	6
Swainson's Thrush		X	X											2
Hermit Thrush	X	X	X	X						X		X		6
American Robin	X	X		X				X				X		5
Varied Thrush	X				X							X		3
Orange-crowned Warbler	X	X	X	X	X	X		X	X			X	X	10
Yellow Warbler	X	X		X										3
Yellow-rumped Warbler	X	X	X	X	X	X		X		X		X		9
Blackpoll Warbler	X	X	X	X	X	X	X			X		X	X	10
Northern Waterthrush	X	X	X	X	X	X	X		X		X	X	X	11
Wilson's Warbler	X	X	X	X	X	X	X	X	X	X		X	X	12
American Tree Sparrow	X	X	X	X	X	X	X	X	X			X	X	11
Savannah Sparrow	X	X	X	X	X	X		X	X	X		X	X	11
Fox Sparrow	X	X		X	X	X			X	X		X	X	9
Lincoln's Sparrow			X	X					X					3
White-crowned Sparrow	X	X	X	X	X	X	X	X	X	X		X		11

Common Name	Grid Number									River Day Number				Number of Detections
	3	4	11	12	21	23	24	29	30	R1	R2	R3	R4	
Golden-crowned Sparrow	X	X	X	X	X					X			X	7
Dark-eyed Junco	X	X	X	X	X									5
Rusty Blackbird								X	X				X	3
Pine Grosbeak	X													1
White-winged Crossbill	X	X	X	X	X	X								6
Redpoll species	X	X	X		X	X						X		6
Pine Siskin	X	X												2
Total number of species	37	33	30	37	30	13	7	27	27	20	6	28	22	

NPS 193/116866, September 2012